Kids' Canadian Atlas

Written and designed by

Nicola Wright • Tony Potter • Christine Wilson • Dee Turner • Chris Leishman

Illustrated by

Lyn Mitchell

Contents

Whitecap Books Ltd.
Vancouver/Toronto

All about maps

A map is a picture of a place from above. Imagine what your home would look like if you flew over it in an airplane and took a photograph. The picture would show the area around your home spread out flat.

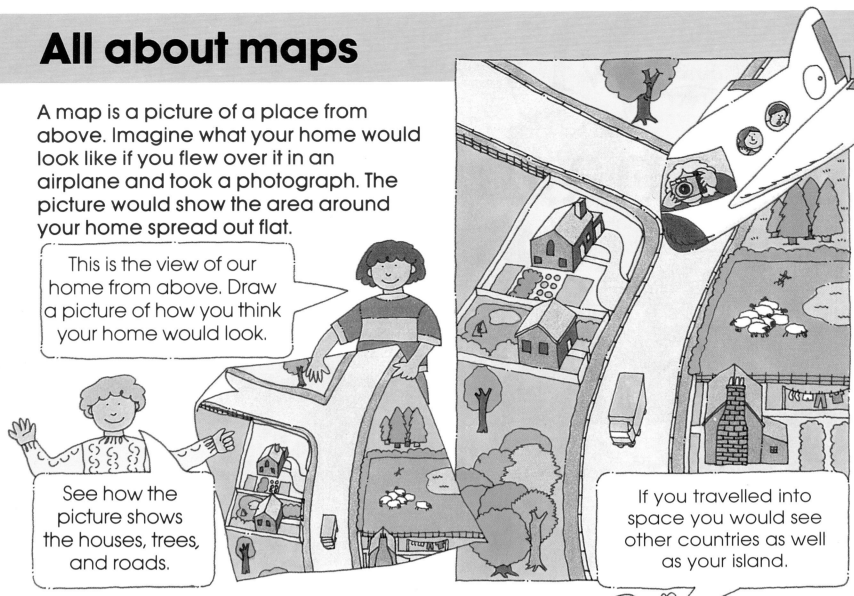

This is the view of our home from above. Draw a picture of how you think your home would look.

See how the picture shows the houses, trees, and roads.

If you travelled into space you would see other countries as well as your island.

My town

My island

The Earth

Imagine that you fly higher. Now you can see your whole town or city. Everything looks tiny.

Imagine your town is on an island. As you go even higher you can see the whole island.

Clouds form in the sky and swirl around the Earth. There is much more ocean than land.

This is how my island would look as a map. Tiny pictures called symbols are used to stand for real things.

2

The pictures below are the symbols used in this book. This part of an atlas is called the **legend**. The legend tells you what the symbols stand for.

Looking for a country? Here is what to do: Go to the list on page 40 and look under the first letter of the country name. So, **Chile** is under the letter **C**.

 Country boundaries

 Oceans and Seas

 Capital cities ■Moscow

Large cities ●Vladivostok

 Lakes

Rivers

 High mountains

Low mountains

 Tropical rain forest

 Monsoon woodland (hot areas with a rainy season)

Pine forest

 Leafy woodland

 Mixed woodland

Mediterranean woodland (dry areas with evergreen trees)

Desert (some deserts are just sandy, but some are stony and covered with bushes or cacti)

Grassland (called **prairie** in North America, and **pampas** in South America)

Steppe (scrubland or grassland in Asia)

Savannah (dry grasslands with some trees in Africa)

Tundra (frozen land)

Ice

World map

This big map shows the world as though its round shape has been flattened out. The differently colored areas of land are called continents. There are seven continents and four oceans.

This is planet Earth. Imagine a line around its middle. This is called the equator.

This book shows you some of the people, animals, plants, and places found in each continent.

The biggest continent is Asia. The smallest continent is Australia.

Countries

The maps in this book show all the countries in the world. A white line shows where one country joins another.

Every country has a flag. Some of them are shown in this book.

The Polish flag

The Belgian flag

Portugal

The Italian flag

The bottom half of the world is called the southern hemisphere.

Arcti Ocean

North America

Atlantic Ocean

Equator

Pacific Ocean

South America

Atlantic Ocean

SOUTH POLE

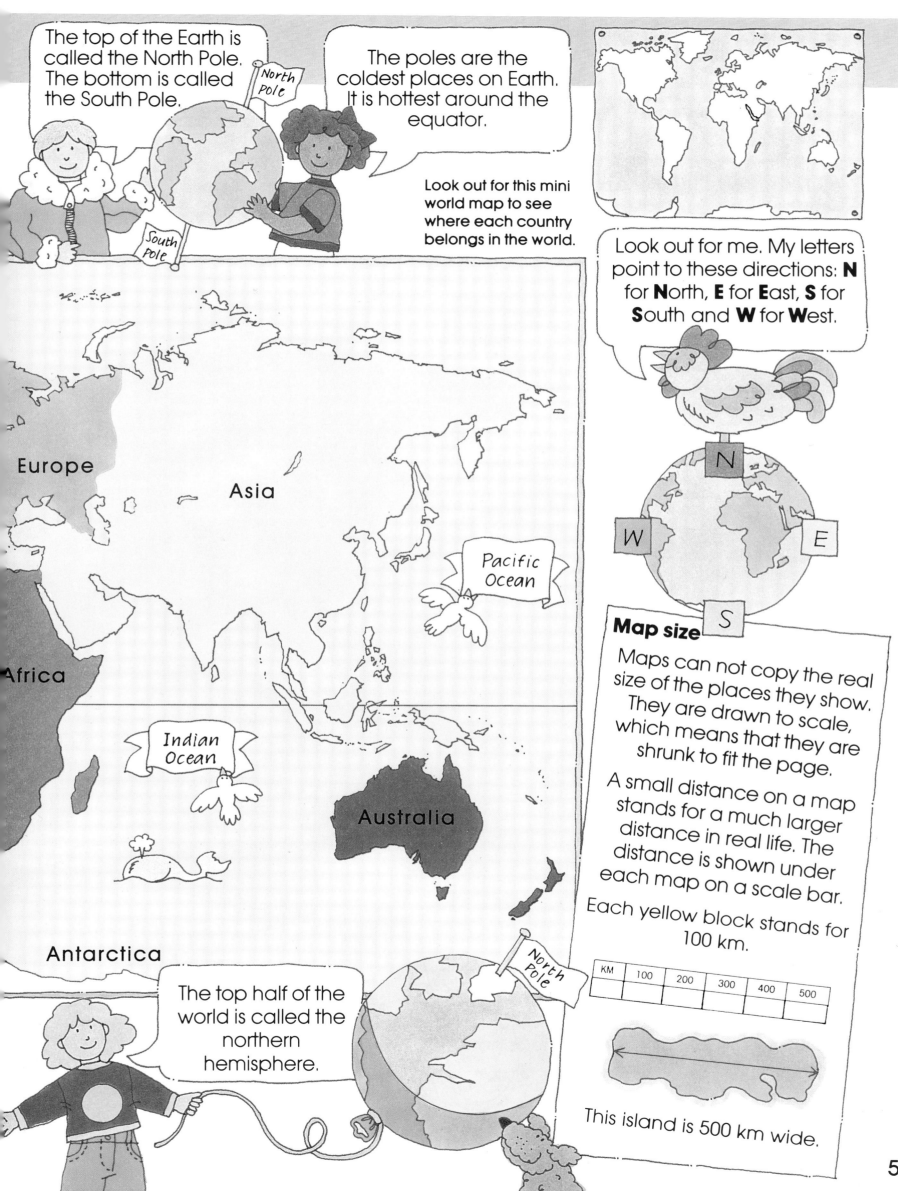

The top of the Earth is called the North Pole. The bottom is called the South Pole.

North Pole

South Pole

The poles are the coldest places on Earth. It is hottest around the equator.

Look out for this mini world map to see where each country belongs in the world.

Look out for me. My letters point to these directions: **N** for **N**orth, **E** for **E**ast, **S** for **S**outh and **W** for **W**est.

N
W   E
S

Europe

Asia

Africa

Pacific Ocean

Indian Ocean

Australia

Antarctica

The top half of the world is called the northern hemisphere.

North Pole

Map size

Maps can not copy the real size of the places they show. They are drawn to scale, which means that they are shrunk to fit the page.

A small distance on a map stands for a much larger distance in real life. The distance is shown under each map on a scale bar.

Each yellow block stands for 100 km.

KM	100	200	300	400	500

This island is 500 km wide.

Canada

Canada is the second largest country in the world. It is divided into ten provinces and three territories. Each province and territory has a capital city. On the map, these capitals are marked with a small star. Ottawa, the capital city of Canada, is marked with a large star. More than 30 million people live in Canada.

Canada's vast northern territories – Yukon, the Northwest Territories, and Nunavut – extend far to the north. Few people live in the far north.

Pacific Ocean

The Rocky Mountains form what is called the Continental Divide. Rivers run down one side of the Rockies to the Pacific Ocean, and down the other side to the Arctic and Atlantic oceans.

YUKON
★ WHITEHORSE

Mackenzie River

Great Bear Lake

NORTHWEST TERRITORIES

YELLOWKNIFE
★

Great Slave Lake

NUNAVUT

C A N A

Prince Rupert

Rocky

Peace River

Lake Athabasca

BRITISH COLUMBIA

ALBERTA

EDMONTON
★

SASKATCHEWAN

MANITOB

Lake Winnipeg

Mountains

Vancouver

Calgary

Saskatoon

REGINA
★

WINNIPEG
★

VICTORIA
★

Manitoba, Saskatchewan and Alberta are called the Prairie Provinces. The land of these provinces is flat and good for farming.

Alberta Saskatchewan Manitoba Ontario Québec Nova Scotia New Brunswick Prince Edward Island

Lake Superior

Canada

Lake Huron

Lake Michigan

Lake Ontario

United States

Lake Erie

The Great Lakes are big lakes along the boundary of Ontario and the United States. The lakes are connected to the Atlantic Ocean by the St. Lawrence Seaway and river.

IQUALUIT

Atlantic Ocean

Newfoundland was the first part of Canada explored by European sailors. The province has two parts – the island of Newfoundland and Labrador on the mainland.

Goose Bay

NEWFOUNDLAND AND LABRADOR

ST JOHN'S

QUÉBEC

CHARLOTTETOWN

P.E.I.

QUÉBEC

NEW BRUNSWICK

NOVA SCOTIA

Nova Scotia, New Brunswick and Prince Edward Island are the Maritime Provinces.

FREDERICTON

HALIFAX

Montreal

OTTAWA

TARIO

TORONTO

Québec is the largest province. Most people who live here speak French. English and French are the official languages of Canada.

Ontario is the second largest province. More people live in Ontario han any other province – over 11 million.

7

The story of Canada

Canada's first people came to North America across the northern part of the continent thousands of years ago.

1497

British explorer John Cabot claimed Newfoundland for England. Viking explorers had been to Newfoundland as early as the 1100s.

1534, 1535 and 1541

During three voyages of exploration for France, Jacques Cartier drew maps of the St. Lawrence area and named it Canada.

1603-1635

Samuel de Champlain helped establish colonies at today's Québec City, and Port-Royal in Nova Scotia.

1791

Most of the early settlers lived along the St. Lawrence River. "Upper Canada" was up the river from "Lower Canada." Upper and Lower Canada were the beginnings of today's provinces of Ontario and Québec.

Settlers followed the early explorers. They began to clear the land and farm it.

Coureurs de bois – runners of the woods – travelled on rivers and lakes in canoes made of birch bark. They bought valuable furs from native people. Fur traders were the first Europeans to explore much of inland Canada.

1792

Captain George Vancouver came to the coast of British Columbia. While the east coast of Canada was being settled by Europeans, the west coast was just beginning to be explored.

On July 1, 1867, the colonies of New Brunswick, Nova Scotia, Ontario and Québec joined together to form the Dominion of Canada. Sir John A. Macdonald was the first prime minister.

1876

The first long-distance telephone call in the world took place in Paris, Ontario. Alexander Graham Bell, inventor of the telephone, called his uncle in Brantford, Ontario.

1880

By 1880, the Dominion of Canada included all of today's Canada, except for Newfoundland, which joined in 1949.

1885

The last spike in the Canadian Pacific Railway was pounded in at Craigellachie, in British Columbia. This important railway linked the settlements, which were few and far apart.

1896

Gold was discovered on the Klondike River in the Yukon. Prospectors rushed in from all over the world.

1922

Dr. Frederick Banting discovered that insulin could control diabetes. He received a Nobel Prize for his work.

1981

Canadian scientists developed a special robot arm, called the Canadarm, for the U.S. Space Shuttle. It is 15 metres long and can pick up and repair satellites in space.

Things to See

Niagara Falls, in Ontario, are 675 metres wide – about as wide as five city blocks.

British Columbia's Queen Charlotte Islands are called Haida Gwaii by the native Haida people. There you can see tall poles, beautifully painted and carved by Haida artists.

The Rockies have some of the highest mountains in Canada.

Prince Edward Island is the setting for Anne of Green Gables, a story written by Lucy Maud Montgomery in 1908. Visitors come from all over the world to see the cottage used as the model for Green Gables.

You can ride in a horse-drawn carriage around the beautiful city of Québec.

Many dinosaur bones have been found in the Badlands area of southern Alberta, near Drumheller. You can see real fossils and life-size replicas of these huge extinct animals.

The CN Tower in Toronto is 553 metres high – one of the highest free-standing structures in the world.

What people do

The flat prairies have rich soil that is good for growing wheat and other grains.

"Bush pilots" fly small airplanes that take people into remote parts of Canada.

Apples, cherries, peaches and grapes are grown in the Okanagan Valley, in British Columbia, and the southern parts of Ontario.

In Alberta, there are many cattle ranches. There are also ranches in the interior of British Columbia.

Miners remove ore, such as iron, copper, coal, gold, zinc, nickel and silver from Canada's rocky areas.

Forestry is an important industry in Canada. The trees are used for both lumber and paper.

Prince Edward Island is famous for its potato crops. It is sometimes called Spud Island.

Salmon, cod, lobster, shrimp and crab are among the seafood caught on the Atlantic and Pacific coasts.

Canada's great natural beauty attracts a lot of travellers. Many people work in hotels and restaurants, or as guides to out-of-the-way places.

Wildlife

Canada has huge areas where few people live, so there are many animals.

Canada geese fly in V-shaped formations. They are the most common geese in Canada.

Deer are found all across Canada. In the spring the fawns are born.

The bald eagle is usually found near water. It builds its huge nest high in a tree. The nest can be up to 3 metres across and weigh as much as a small car.

Prairie dogs and gophers live mostly underground, where they dig complex tunnels. Mounds of dirt mark the entrances to their burrows.

Wolves are found mainly in Canada's north.

The prairies were once the home of herds of bison numbering in the millions. Today small herds are protected in four parks.

Raccoons live across most of southern Canada, even in the cities. Their black face markings look like a mask.

A male moose grows a set of antlers, called a "rack." Each year, until it is about ten, a moose's rack grows larger.

Barrenground caribou are great travellers. Each year they migrate across the Arctic along trails they have followed for centuries.

Canada has many bears. Black bears live in the forests across Canada. Grizzlies are huge bears that occupy more remote regions. The polar bear lives in the far north.

Seals, like whales, are marine mammals. You can often see harbour seals around docks and shorelines.

Killer whales, or orcas, have beautiful black and white markings. They are often seen on the Pacific and Atlantic coasts. They usually travel in family groups called pods.

Beluga whales are completely white. Large amounts of blubber help them survive in the cold Arctic waters where they live.

North America

North America contains Canada, the United States of America, Mexico, and the countries of Central America. Canada is the second largest country in the world. The U.S. is the fourth largest and has fifty states.

The Canadian flag

Ice hockey is a very popular sport in Canada.

Skiing is popular in the Rocky mountains. The Rockies run from Canada, through the United States.

Alaska (USA)

Yukon River

Alaskan Mountains

Fairbanks

Anchorage

Great Bear Lake

Great Slave Lake

Canadian police are called Mounties. Some still ride horses, but most drive cars or motorcycles

The U.S. produces more timber than any other country.

Lake Athabasca

Rocky Mountains

Vancouver

Columbia River

Snake River

Fact file

 Highest mountain: Mount Mckinley, Alaska, 6,194 m.

Longest river: Mississippi-Missouri River, U.S., 6,212 km.

Largest lake: Lake Superior, U.S.-Canada, is the second largest in the world. 82,383 sq km.

Weather: Canada and Alaska are colder than the rest of North America.

Biggest city: Mexico City, Mexico, about 14 million people.

Number of people: Canada about 31 million. U.S., about 285 million. Mexico, about 100 million. Costa Rica, about 4 million. Panama, about 3 million.

One of the world's most active volcanos, Mauna Loa, is in Hawaii.

Hawaii (USA)

Sierra Nevada

Colorado River

Los Angeles
San Diego

The American flag

Pacific Ocean

The Aztecs were a civilization in Mexico hundreds of years ago. Mexicans are proud of their Aztec ancestry.

Bananas, coffee, and sugar are grown in Central America.

The Mexican flag

KM	250	500	1000	1500	2000	2500	3000	3500	4000	4500	5000	5500	6000	6500

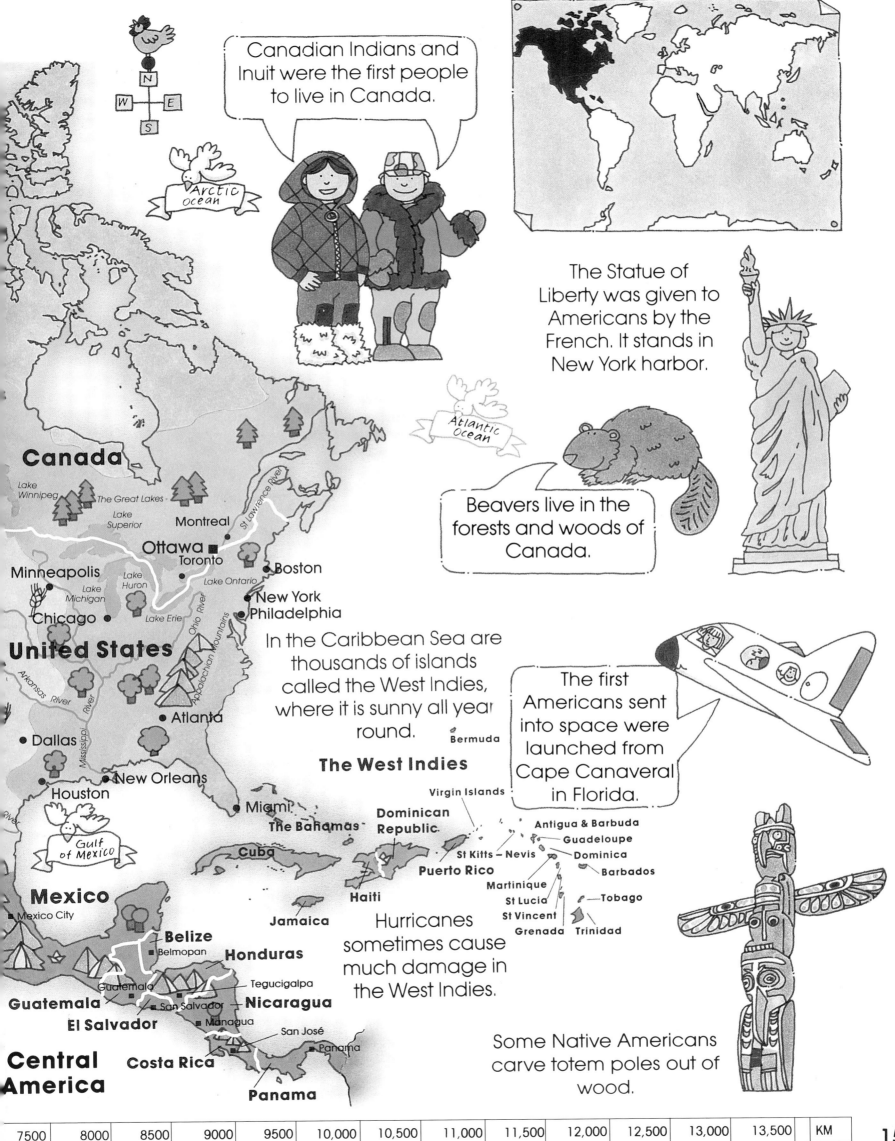

Canadian Indians and Inuit were the first people to live in Canada.

Arctic Ocean

The Statue of Liberty was given to Americans by the French. It stands in New York harbor.

Atlantic Ocean

Beavers live in the forests and woods of Canada.

Canada

Lake Winnipeg
The Great Lakes
Lake Superior
Montreal
St Lawrence River
Ottawa
Toronto
Minneapolis
Lake Huron
Lake Michigan
Lake Ontario
Boston
Lake Erie
New York
Chicago
Philadelphia

United States

Ohio River
Appalachian Mountains
Arkansas River
Mississippi River
Atlanta
Dallas
New Orleans
Houston

In the Caribbean Sea are thousands of islands called the West Indies, where it is sunny all year round.

Bermuda

The West Indies

The first Americans sent into space were launched from Cape Canaveral in Florida.

Gulf of Mexico

Miami
The Bahamas
Cuba

Mexico

Mexico City

Virgin Islands
Dominican Republic
Puerto Rico
Haiti
Jamaica

Antigua & Barbuda
Guadeloupe
St Kitts – Nevis
Dominica
Barbados
Martinique
St Lucia
Tobago
St Vincent
Grenada
Trinidad

Belize
Belmopan
Honduras
Guatemala
Tegucigalpa
Guatemala
Nicaragua
San Salvador
El Salvador
Managua
San José
Panama

Hurricanes sometimes cause much damage in the West Indies.

Central America

Costa Rica

Panama

Some Native Americans carve totem poles out of wood.

7500	8000	8500	9000	9500	10,000	10,500	11,000	11,500	12,000	12,500	13,000	13,500	KM

South America

South America is the fourth largest continent. It is made up of 13 different countries. There are mountains and rain forests as well as plains and deserts. The weather ranges from very hot to very cold.

The Brazilian flag

Galapagos Islands

Hummingbirds are found in rain forests. They are very tiny and brightly colored.

Anteaters also live in the rain forests. They use their long, sticky tongues to eat ants.

Rubber trees grow in South America. The tree bark is cut and the sticky sap runs out. It is collected to make rubber products.

Llamas are used to carry things in the Andes. Their thick fur protects them from the cold.

Copper mines in northern Chile supply the world with copper.

The Chilean flag

The Ecuador f

Caracas

Venezuela

Orinoco River

Guyana
Suriname
French Guiana

Angel Falls

Georgetown

Guiana Highlands

Paramaribo

Cayenne

Bogota

Colombia

Quito

Ecuador

Amazon River

Manaos

Lima

Peru

Bolivia

La Paz

Paraguay River

Brasili

Chile

Paraguay

Asuncion

Parana River

Andes Mountains

Santiago

Buenos Aires

Uruguay

Montevideo

Argentina

Falkland Islands

KM	250	500	1000	1500	2000	2500	3000	3500	4000	4500	5000	5500

The world's biggest bird, the condor, is found in South America. Its wings measure 9 feet across.

Patterns like these are woven into fabric by South American Indians.

Brazil

Brazilian Highlands

Recife •

São Francisco River

Salvador

Atlantic Ocean

The Incas built huge forts and temples more than 500 years ago in the Andes mountains. The ruins of their buildings can still be seen.

o de neiro

The Bolivian flag

Fierce piranha live in the Amazon River.

Argentina has some of the largest cattle farms in the world. The cows are looked after by South American cowboys called gauchos.

Fact file

Highest mountains: The Andes, over, 6,949 m.

Longest river: The Amazon is the second longest river in the world, 6,738 km.

Largest lake: Lake Titicaca, Peru-Bolivia, 8,300 sq km.

Highest waterfall: Angel Falls, in Venezuela is the highest in the world, 979 m.

Biggest city: Sao Paulo, about 16 million people.

Number of people in some countries: Chile, about 15 million. Argentina, about 37 million. Brazil, about 172 million.

The Colombian flag

The Peruvian flag

The Venezuelan flag

| 6500 | 7000 | 7500 | 8000 | 8500 | 9000 | 9500 | 10,000 | 10,500 | 11,000 | 11,500 | KM |

Northern Europe

These northern European countries are known as Scandinavia. Norway has over 150,000 islands along its coastline. The Norwegian coast is jagged, with deep inlets called fjords. Forests and lakes cover large areas of Scandinavia. Many bears and wolves used to live in the forests.

Workers travel to the oil rigs by helicopter.

Children here learn to ski almost as soon as they can walk!

There is oil under the sea bed. Oil rigs are used to pump the oil up to the surface.

The oil is used as fuel for cars and for heating buildings.

Trawlers are fishing boats that catch fish by dragging nets along the sea bed. Many Norwegian fishing boats fish in the North Sea.

Some fishing boats can stay out at sea for months at a time.

The Danish flag

The Norwegian flag

Norwegian Sea

North Sea

Bodo

Trondheim

River Glama

Norway

River Klaralven

Bergen

Stavanger

Oslo

Sweden

Lake Vanern

Stockholm

Alan Islan

Gothenburg

Lake Vattern

Jonkoping

Gotland

Denmark

Oland

Malmo

Copenhagen

Bornholm

Baltic Sea

KM	250	500	1000

Herds of reindeer live in the forests of the far North.

In summer in the far North it never gets dark, even at night.

The forest trees are cut down and used to make houses, furniture and paper.

The Finnish flag

The Swedish flag

Lapland

Lake Inari

Gulf of Bothnia

Finland

• Tampere

Helsinki

Seals live in the Gulf of Bothnia.

Logs are floated down rivers to sawmills.

Finland has more than 50,000 lakes. Sweden has nearly 96,000 lakes!

Fact file

Highest mountain: Mount Glittertind, Norway, 2,472 m.

Longest river: Glåma River, Norway, 611 km.

Weather: Scandinavia has long, cold, dark winters and short, mild summers.

Biggest city: Stockholm, Sweden, about 2 million people.

Number of people: Finland, about 5 million. Norway, about 4 million. Sweden, about 8 million. Denmark, about 5 million.

Britain and Central Europe

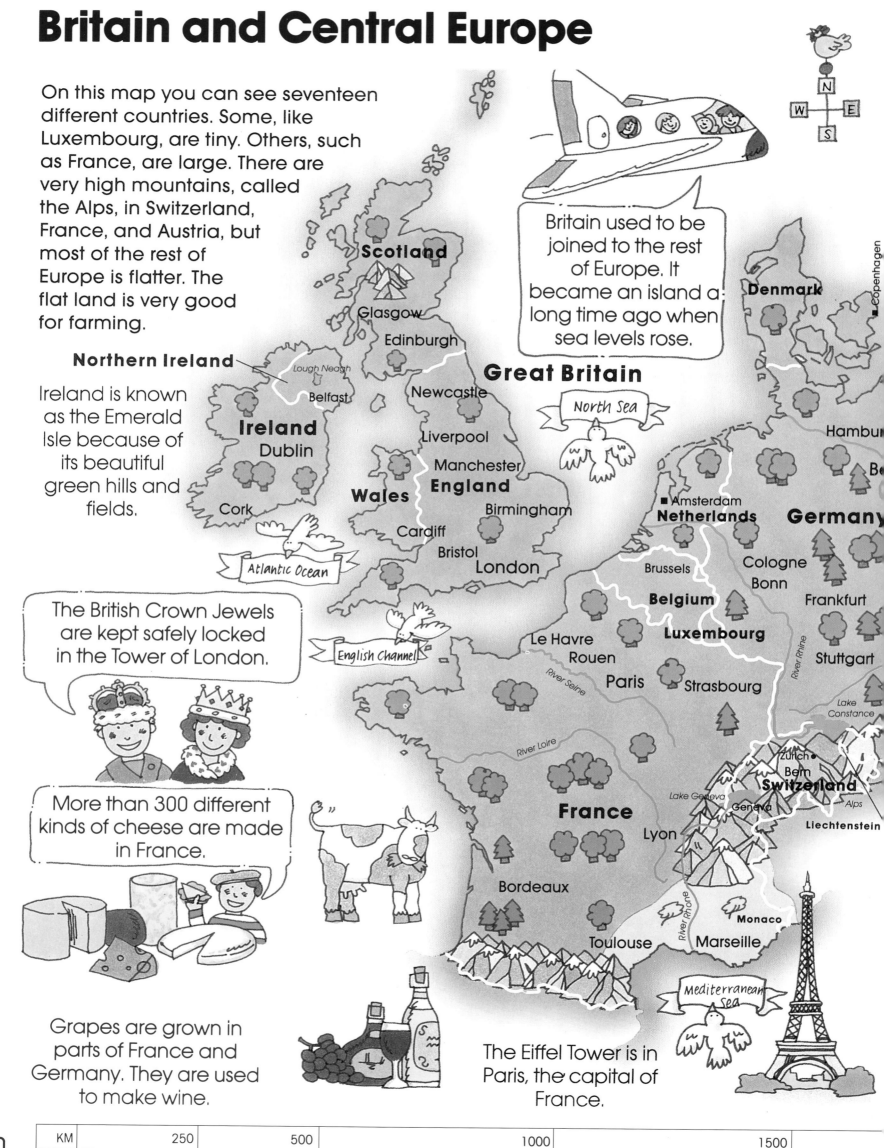

On this map you can see seventeen different countries. Some, like Luxembourg, are tiny. Others, such as France, are large. There are very high mountains, called the Alps, in Switzerland, France, and Austria, but most of the rest of Europe is flatter. The flat land is very good for farming.

Northern Ireland

Ireland is known as the Emerald Isle because of its beautiful green hills and fields.

Britain used to be joined to the rest of Europe. It became an island a long time ago when sea levels rose.

The British Crown Jewels are kept safely locked in the Tower of London.

More than 300 different kinds of cheese are made in France.

Grapes are grown in parts of France and Germany. They are used to make wine.

The Eiffel Tower is in Paris, the capital of France.

Scotland
Glasgow
Edinburgh
Lough Neagh
Belfast
Newcastle
Great Britain
Denmark
Copenhagen
North Sea
Ireland
Dublin
Liverpool
Manchester
England
Hamburg
Cork
Wales
Birmingham
Cardiff
Bristol
London
Amsterdam
Netherlands
Germany
Brussels
Cologne
Bonn
Belgium
Frankfurt
Luxembourg
River Rhine
Stuttgart
Le Havre
Rouen
River Seine
Paris
Strasbourg
Lake Constance
Atlantic Ocean
English Channel
River Loire
Zurich
Bern
Switzerland
Lake Geneva
Geneva
Alps
Liechtenstein
France
Lyon
Bordeaux
Monaco
River Rhône
Toulouse
Marseille
Mediterranean Sea

KM	250	500	1000	1500

The Netherlands are so low and flat that the sea can flood in. Sea walls protect the land and windmills pump water away. Many Dutch farmers grow flowers.

The Swiss flag *The British Union Jack* *The French flag*

Germany, France, and Britain have big factories making many things from cars to computers.

The German flag *The Austrian flag*

Gdansk

River Vistula

Warsaw

Poznan

Poland

River Oder

Wroclaw

River Elbe

Krakow

Carpathians

ue

Czech Republic **Slovakia**

Vienna Bratislava

Budapest

Hungary

Salzburg

River Danube

Austria

Cluj-Napoca

Romania

Constanta

Timisoara **Bucharest**

Fact file

🏔 *Highest mountain:* Mont Blanc, France, 4,801 m.

🏞 *Longest river:* The Danube, 2,858 km.

⛅ *Weather:* Most of this part of Europe has mild winters and cool summers. Rain falls all year round. Snow falls in many places in winter.

🏙 *Biggest city:* Paris, France, about 10 million people.

👥 *Number of people in some European countries:* France, about 59 million. Great Britain (England, Scotland and Wales), about 59 million. Germany, about 82 million. Netherlands, about 16 million. Luxembourg, about 443,000

Bulgaria

Sofia

Skiing is a popular sport in the mountains.

There are many fairytale castles built along the banks of the Rhine River in Germany.

Mediterranean Europe

The countries around the Mediterranean Sea are sunny all year. Olives, fruit, and vegetables are grown in all these countries. Many people go to the Mediterranean for vacations. In parts of Spain and Italy there are high mountains where people ski in the winter.

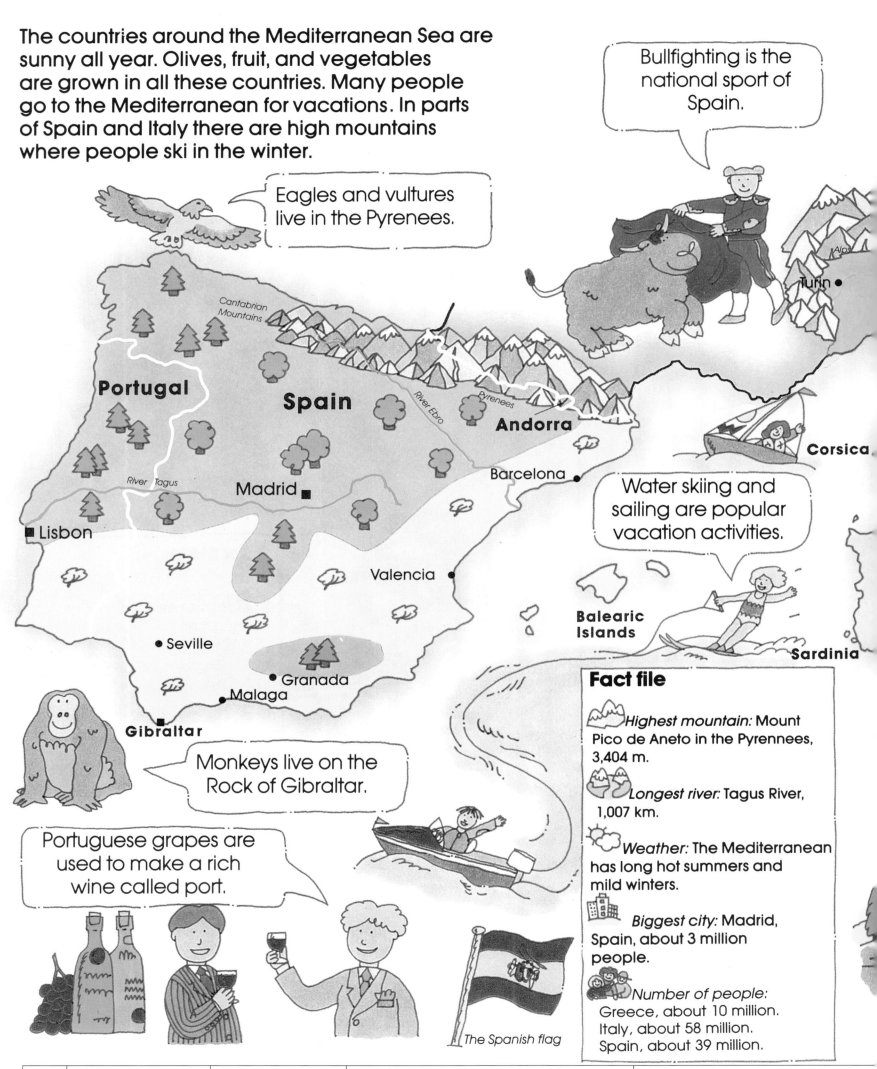

Bullfighting is the national sport of Spain.

Eagles and vultures live in the Pyrenees.

Cantabrian Mountains

Portugal

Spain

River Ebro

Pyrenees

Andorra

Alps

Turin •

Corsica

Barcelona •

Water skiing and sailing are popular vacation activities.

River Tagus

Madrid ■

• Lisbon

Valencia •

Balearic Islands

Sardinia

• Seville

• Granada

• Malaga

Gibraltar

Monkeys live on the Rock of Gibraltar.

Portuguese grapes are used to make a rich wine called port.

The Spanish flag

Fact file

Highest mountain: Mount Pico de Aneto in the Pyrennees, 3,404 m.

Longest river: Tagus River, 1,007 km.

Weather: The Mediterranean has long hot summers and mild winters.

Biggest city: Madrid, Spain, about 3 million people.

Number of people: Greece, about 10 million. Italy, about 58 million. Spain, about 39 million.

KM		250	500		1000

Venice is built on many small islands in the sea. Many of the streets are canals, so people travel around the city in boats.

The herds of goats and sheep in the mountains provide milk, cheese, wool, butter, and meat.

Most of Italy's factories are in the north of the country.

The Leaning Tower of Pisa in Italy has been leaning ever since it was built over 600 years ago.

There are over 1,400 Greek islands.

Many people in southern Italy are farmers.

The Ancient Greeks and Romans built many fine temples and buildings. Today tourists go to see the ruins.

The Greek flag

The Italian flag

Dolomites
Venice
Ljubljana
Slovenia
Zagreb
Croatia
Bosnia & Herzegovina
Belgrade
River Po
San Marino
Florence
Pisa
Serbia
Italy
Sarajevo
Montenegro
Titograd
Adriatic Sea
Skopje
Rome
Macedonia
Naples
Tirane
Albania
Pindus Mountains
Turkey
Greece
Athens
Sicily
Crete
Malta

2000   2500   KM   23

Africa

Africa is the second largest continent in the world. It is split up into lots of different countries. Most of Africa is covered in grassland and desert. Some of the tropical rain forests in Africa have been chopped down to build villages and farms.

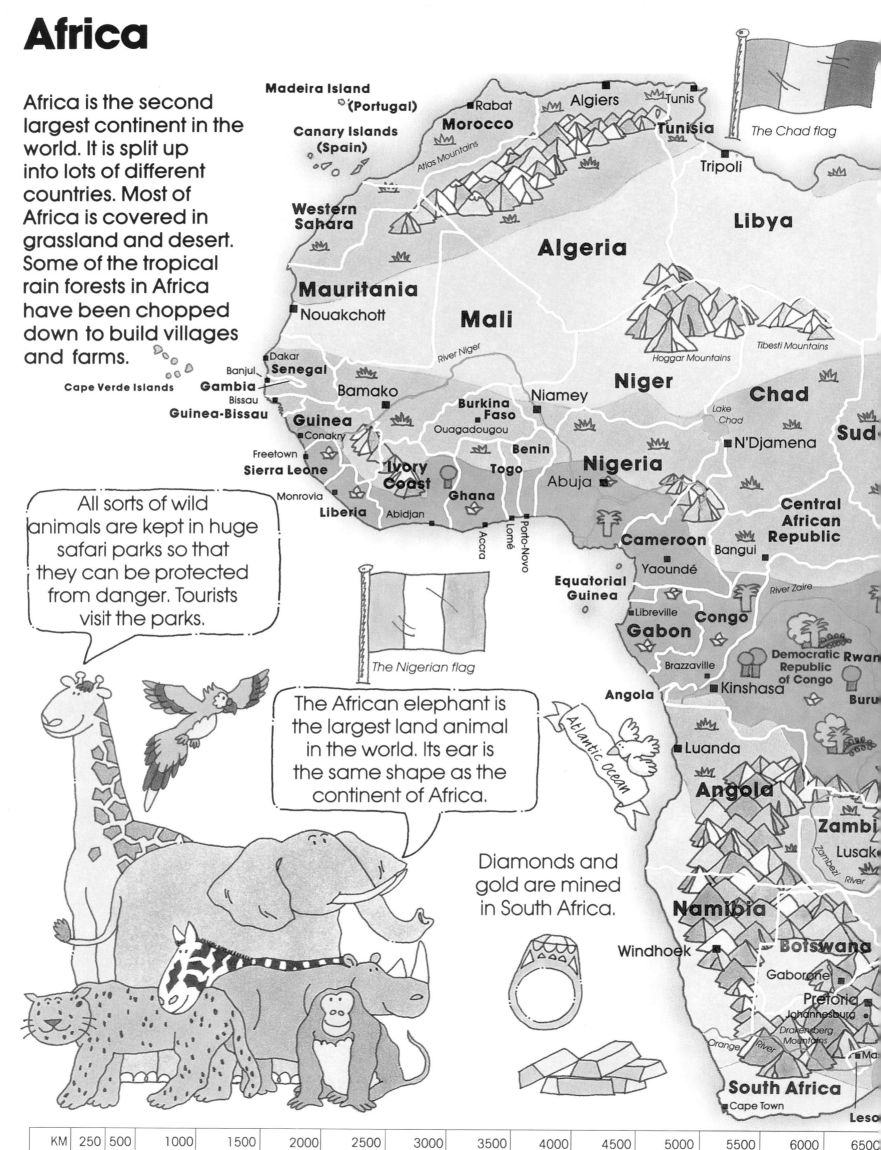

All sorts of wild animals are kept in huge safari parks so that they can be protected from danger. Tourists visit the parks.

The African elephant is the largest land animal in the world. Its ear is the same shape as the continent of Africa.

Diamonds and gold are mined in South Africa.

The Chad flag

The Nigerian flag

Atlantic Ocean

Madeira Island (Portugal)
Canary Islands (Spain)
Cape Verde Islands

Rabat
Morocco
Algiers
Tunis
Tunisia
Atlas Mountains
Tripoli
Libya

Western Sahara
Algeria

Mauritania
Nouakchott

Mali

River Niger

Hoggar Mountains
Tibesti Mountains

Dakar
Banjul
Senegal
Gambia
Bissau
Guinea-Bissau
Bamako

Niger
Niamey
Chad
Lake Chad
N'Djamena
Sud

Guinea
Conakry
Burkina Faso
Ouagadougou
Benin
Nigeria
Abuja
Central African Republic

Freetown
Sierra Leone
Monrovia
Liberia
Ivory Coast
Ghana
Abidjan
Togo
Accra
Lomé
Porto-Novo

Cameroon
Bangui
Yaoundé

Equatorial Guinea

Libreville
Gabon
Congo
River Zaire

Brazzaville
Democratic Republic of Congo
Rwan
Kinshasa
Buru

Angola
Luanda

Angola

Zambi
Lusak
Zambezi River

Namibia
Windhoek
Botswana
Gaborone

Pretoria
Johannesburg
Drakensberg Mountains
Orange River
Ma

South Africa
Cape Town
Leso

	KM	250	500	1000	1500	2000	2500	3000	3500	4000	4500	5000	5500	6000	6500

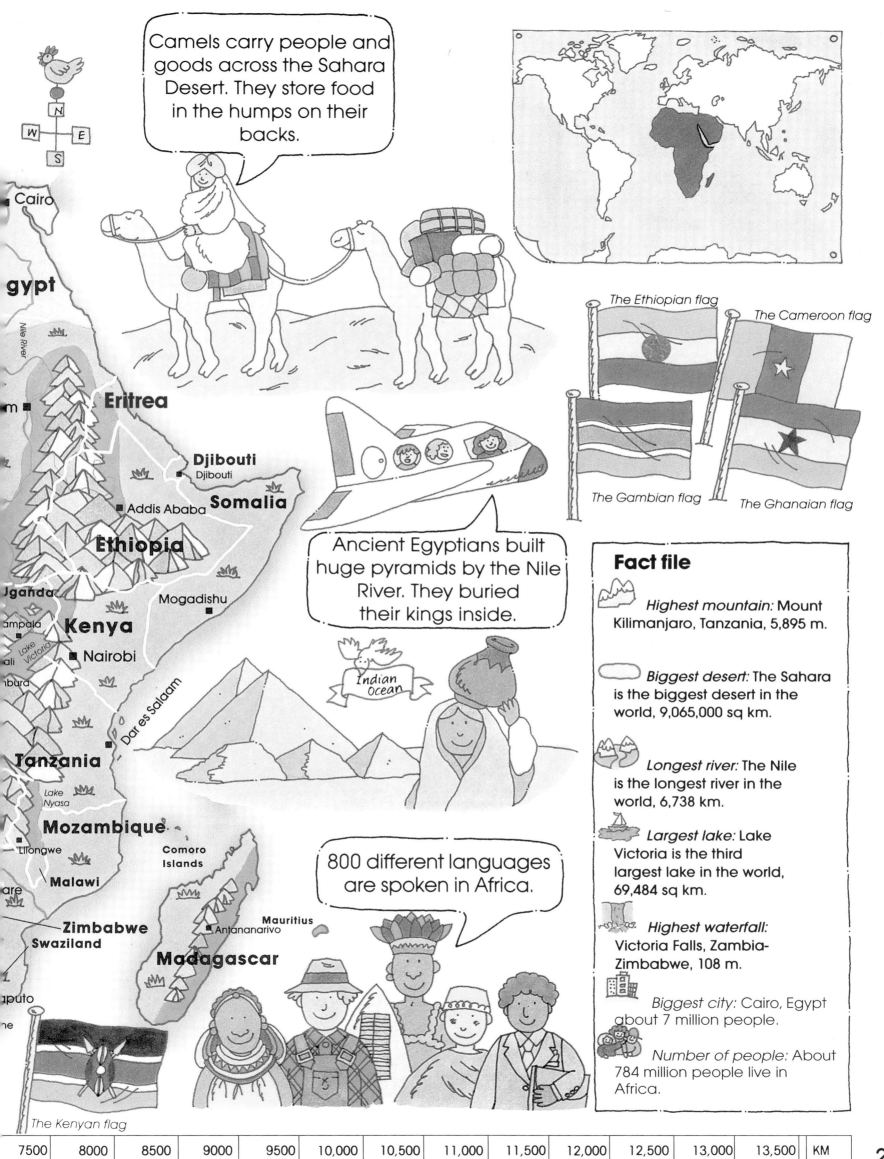

Camels carry people and goods across the Sahara Desert. They store food in the humps on their backs.

Cairo

Egypt

Nile River

Eritrea

Djibouti
Djibouti

Addis Ababa

Somalia

Ethiopia

Uganda

Mogadishu

Kampala

Kenya

Lake Victoria

Nairobi

Mbura

Dar es Salaam

Tanzania

Lake Nyasa

Mozambique

Lilongwe

Comoro Islands

Malawi

Harare

Zimbabwe
Antananarivo

Mauritius

Swaziland

Madagascar

Maputo

The Kenyan flag

The Ethiopian flag

The Cameroon flag

The Gambian flag

The Ghanaian flag

Ancient Egyptians built huge pyramids by the Nile River. They buried their kings inside.

Indian Ocean

800 different languages are spoken in Africa.

Fact file

Highest mountain: Mount Kilimanjaro, Tanzania, 5,895 m.

Biggest desert: The Sahara is the biggest desert in the world, 9,065,000 sq km.

Longest river: The Nile is the longest river in the world, 6,738 km.

Largest lake: Lake Victoria is the third largest lake in the world, 69,484 sq km.

Highest waterfall: Victoria Falls, Zambia-Zimbabwe, 108 m.

Biggest city: Cairo, Egypt about 7 million people.

Number of people: About 784 million people live in Africa.

| 7500 | 8000 | 8500 | 9000 | 9500 | 10,000 | 10,500 | 11,000 | 11,500 | 12,000 | 12,500 | 13,000 | 13,500 | KM |

The Former U.S.S.R.

In 1991 the former U.S.S.R. (the Soviet Union) broke up into 15 separate republics. Estonia, Lithuania and Latvia became fully independent. Most of the other republics agreed to work together in a Commonwealth.

The north is freezing cold, but the deserts in the south are burning hot. In between there are forests and farmlands.

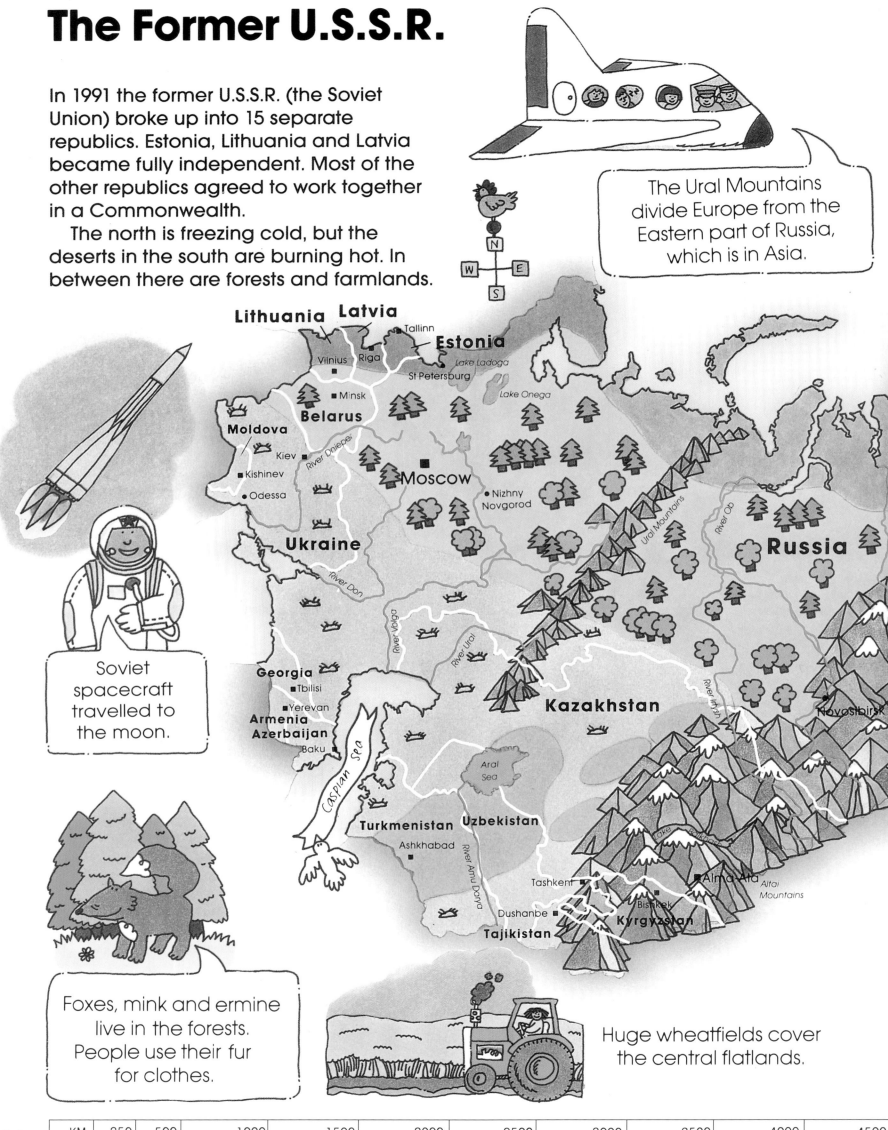

The Ural Mountains divide Europe from the Eastern part of Russia, which is in Asia.

Soviet spacecraft travelled to the moon.

Foxes, mink and ermine live in the forests. People use their fur for clothes.

Huge wheatfields cover the central flatlands.

Lithuania · Latvia · Tallinn · Estonia · Vilnius · Riga · Lake Ladoga · St Petersburg · Lake Onega · Minsk · Belarus · Moldova · Kiev · River Dniepei · Moscow · Nizhny Novgorod · Kishinev · Odessa · Ukraine · River Don · River Volga · River Ural · Ural Mountains · River Ob · Russia · River Irtysh · Novosibirsk · Georgia · Tbilisi · Yerevan · Armenia · Azerbaijan · Baku · Caspian Sea · Kazakhstan · Aral Sea · Turkmenistan · Uzbekistan · Ashkhabad · River Amu Darya · Tashkent · Lake Balkhash · Alma Ata · Altai Mountains · Bishkek · Dushanbe · Kyrgyzstan · Tajikistan

KM	250	500	1000	1500	2000	2500	3000	3500	4000	4500

Moscow, the capital of Russia, has beautiful old buildings with onion-shaped domes on top.

Arctic Ocean

Bering Sea

Russian dancers, writers and musicians are known all over the world.

Kolyma Mountains

Cherskiy Mountains

Verkhoyansk Mountains

River Lena

Sea of Okhotsk

River Amur

Vladivostok

Many people spend their holidays by the Black Sea.

There are rich supplies of coal, oil and gas under the ground.

Fact file

Highest mountain: Communism Peak, 7,495 m.

Longest river: The Volga, 3,690 km.

Largest city: Moscow, Russia, nearly 9 million.

Weather: In the north there is Arctic ice. In the south there is burning desert. Most places inland have hot summers and cold winters.

Number of people About 290 million.

| 5500 | 6000 | 6500 | 7000 | 7500 | 8000 | 8500 | 9000 | 9500 | KM |

The Middle East

Most of the Middle East is either mountainous or hot, sandy desert. Some of the countries have a great deal of valuable oil under the ground. The oil is pumped up to the surface at oil wells. It is then sold to other countries for use as gasoline and other kinds of fuel.

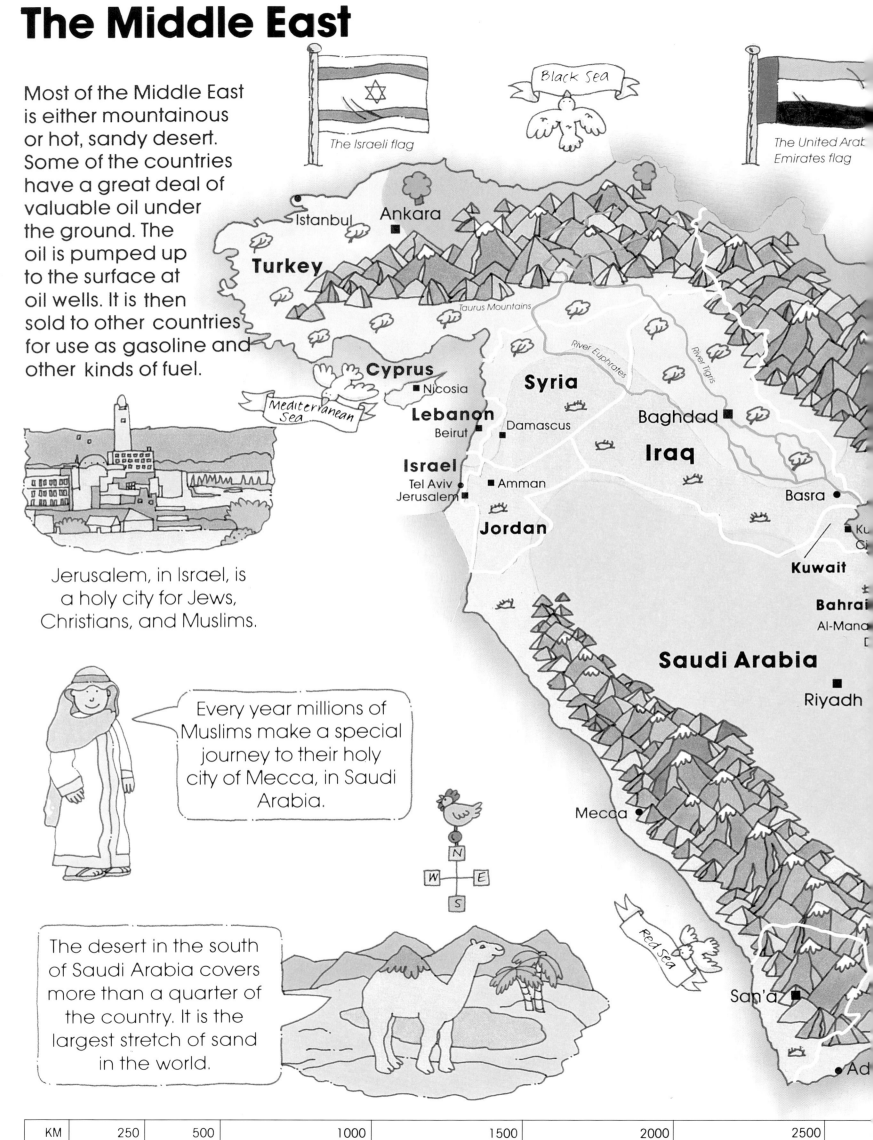

The Israeli flag

Black Sea

The United Arab Emirates flag

Jerusalem, in Israel, is a holy city for Jews, Christians, and Muslims.

Every year millions of Muslims make a special journey to their holy city of Mecca, in Saudi Arabia.

The desert in the south of Saudi Arabia covers more than a quarter of the country. It is the largest stretch of sand in the world.

Istanbul
Ankara
Turkey
Taurus Mountains
Cyprus
Nicosia
Mediterranean Sea
Syria
Lebanon
Beirut
Damascus
River Euphrates
River Tigris
Baghdad
Iraq
Israel
Tel Aviv
Jerusalem
Amman
Basra
Jordan
Kuwait
Bahrai
Al-Mana
Saudi Arabia
Riyadh
N W E S
Mecca
Red Sea
San'a
Ad

KM	250	500	1000	1500	2000	2500

Leopards live in the mountains of Iran.

Afghanistan

■ Kabul

Hindu Kush

Elburz Mountains

ran

Iran

Mountains

The Iranian flag

There is very little rain in these countries. Some water is found in deep underground wells. Seawater can also be purified for drinking.

Persian Gulf

Oman

■ Abu Dhabi

Muscat ■

tar

United Arab Emirates

Nomadic tribes live in parts of Iran. They live in tents, travelling from place to place with their goats and sheep.

Oman

men

The Saudi Arabian flag

Beautiful rugs and carpets are made in Iran.

Oil is carried by pipe line from oil wells to ports. Ships take the oil all over the world.

Fact file

Highest mountains: Elburz Mountains, Iran, over 5,600 m.

Longest river: Euphrates River, 3,597 km.

Weather: These countries have hot summers and cold winters.

Biggest city: Tehran Iran, about 7 million people.

Number of people: Israel, about 6 million. Iran, about 71 million. Iraq, about 23 million. Saudi Arabia, about 21 million.

| 000 | 3500 | 4000 | 4500 | 5000 | 5500 | KM |

South Asia

Much of South Asia is farmland, and relies on the heavy monsoon rains between June and October for crops to grow. The Himalayas are the highest mountain range in the world and divide South Asia from China.

The Himalayas are too icy to cross in winter.

The monsoon rains and storms cause terrible floods, which can destroy whole villages.

The shape of the Indian elephant's ear is the same as the outline of India.

Many people in South Asia eat rice every day.

More tea is grown in India than anywhere else in the world.

Islamabad

Lahore •

Delhi •

New Delhi ■

Nepal

Kathmandu ■

River Indus

Pakistan

Thar desert

Kanpur • River Ganges

Karachi •

• Ahmadabad

India

Bombay

• Hyderabad

Bay of Bengal

The Pakistani flag

Bangalore •

Madras •

The Sri Lankan flag

Colombo ■

Sri Lanka

The Indian flag

KM	250	500	1000	1500	2000	2500

Ponies and yaks are used to carry goods across the Himalayas.

Elephants and tigers live on the lower slopes of the Himalayas and in the swamps of the Ganges River.

India is the second most populous country in the world.

Fact file

⛰️ *Highest mountain:* Mount Everest, 8,848 m.

🏔️ *Longest river:* Ganges-Brahmaputra, 2,900 km.

🌤️ *Weather:* It is very cold in the mountains, but hot most of the year elsewhere.

🏢 *Biggest city:* Calcutta, Iran, about 13 million people.

👨‍👩‍👧 *Number of people in some countries:*
Nepal, about 23 million.
Bangladesh, about 140 million.
Bhutan, about 2 million.
India, about 1 billion.
Sri Lanka, about 19 million.
Pakistan, about 144 million.

Cows are sacred animals in India. They are not kept in fields but are allowed to graze where they like.

Cotton plants produce threads that are made into cotton fabric. It can be painted or dyed and made into clothes.

The Taj Mahal, near Agra in northern India, is often called the most beautiful building in the world.

3000	3500	4000	4500	5000	KM

Southeast Asia

Southeast Asia is an area that curves from Myanmar through a chain of islands towards Australia. It is warm all the year round, but the monsoon wind brings heavy rains. They can damage the traditional houses made of woven palm leaves.

In Thailand, elephants are used to haul trees from the forest to the river, where they float down to the sawmills.

The Thai flag

Coral are sea creatures that live in the warm, shallow waters of the Pacific. When they die, their hard skeletons form islands and reefs. Millions of coral are needed to make one small island.

Fishing is a way of life for many islanders. Their boats are like canoes with small sails.

Coral islands when seen from above have a turquoise band of sea around them.

Mandalay
Myanmar
Rangoon
Irrawaddy River
Laos
Vientiane
Hanoi
Thailand
Bangkok
Vietnam
Cambodia
Phnom Penh
South China Sea
Ho Chi Minh City
Kuala Lumpur
Medan
Malaysia
Brunei
Bandar Seri Begawan
Singapore
Jakarta
Indonesia
Semarang
Surabaya
Bandung

KM	250	500	1000	1500	2000	2500	3000

There are many factories around Manila, but most people live by growing rice and catching fish.

Many of the mountains are volcanoes.

The Philippines are made up of over 7,000 islands.

Quezon City

nila

Philippines

Cebu

The Singaporean flag

A volcano is a hole where molten rock gushes out from under the Earth. So much comes out that new mountains are formed around the hole.

N
W   E
S

Fact file

Highest mountain: Puncak Jaya, Indonesia, 4,884 m.

Longest river: Mekong River, 4,184 km.

Weather: It is hot all year round, with cooling sea breezes. The monsoon wind brings heavy rainfall, and sometimes there are strong winds called typhoons.

Biggest city: Jakarta, Indonesia, about 10 million.

Number of people in some countries: Philippines, about 77 million. Thailand, about 63 million. Malaysia, about 22 million. Indonesia, about 214 million.

Some of the animals in New Guinea are like those in nearby Australia, such as the wallaby.

Papua New Guinea

Indonesia

The Papua New Guinean flag

Port Moresby

| 4000 | 4500 | 5000 | 5500 | 6000 | 6500 | 7000 | KM |

East Asia

China is the third largest country in the world. Japan is much smaller, about the same size as Britain, but it is the richest country in Asia.

Chinese temples and pagodas have tiled roofs that curl up at the corners.

The Mongolian flag

Mongolia

Ulan Bator

Altai Mountains

Gobi Desert

China

Yellow River

Tibetan Plateau

•Taiyu

Himalayas

Tibet

River Mekong

Xian

•Chengdu

River Yangtze

Co

Fact file

Highest mountain: Gosainthan, China, 8,013 m.

Longest river: Yangtze River, China, 5,530 km.

Weather: Northern China and Japan have wet summers and dry winters. The south is warm all year round.

Biggest city: Tokyo, Japan, about 11 million people.

Number of people: Japan, about 127 million. China, about 1.3 billion

The Chinese flag

KM	250	500	1000	1500	2000	2500	300

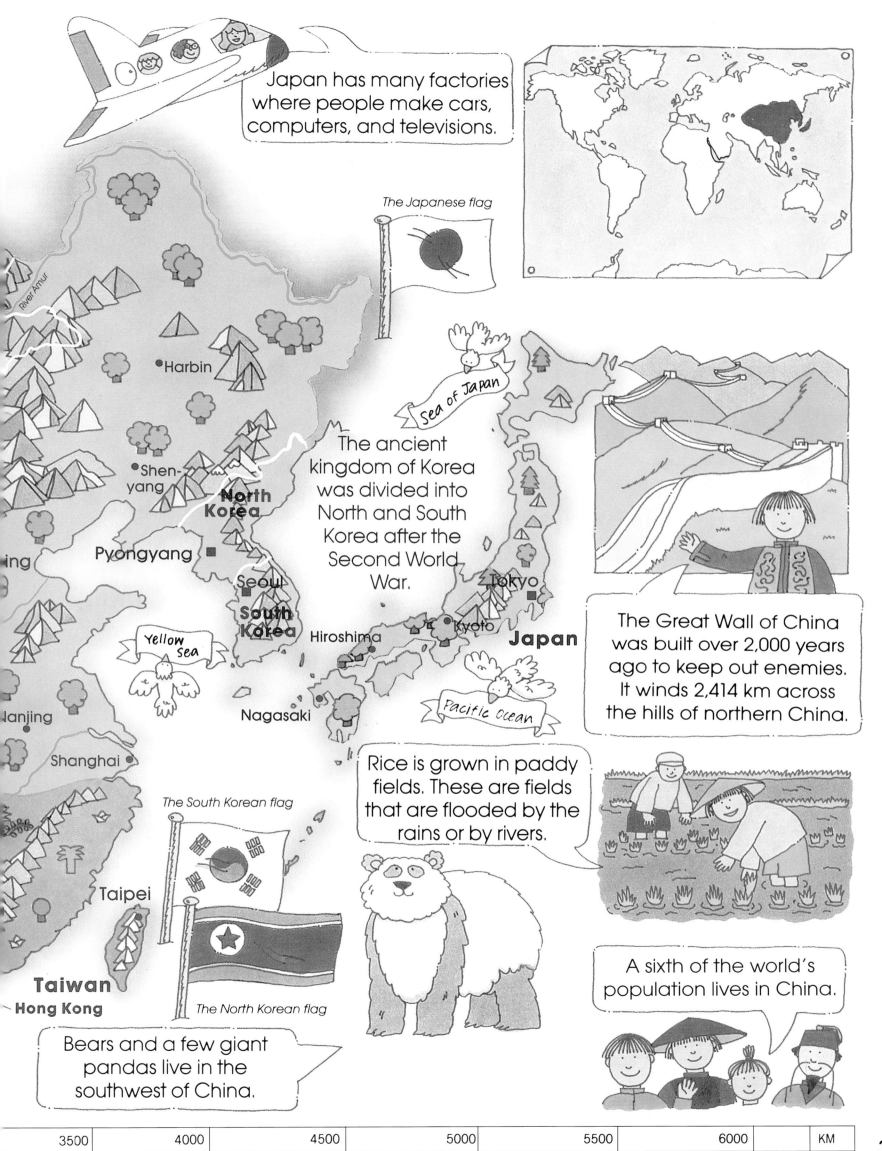

Japan has many factories where people make cars, computers, and televisions.

The Japanese flag

The ancient kingdom of Korea was divided into North and South Korea after the Second World War.

Sea of Japan

Harbin

Shen-yang

North Korea

Pyongyang

Seoul

South Korea

Hiroshima

Yellow Sea

Nanjing

Nagasaki

Shanghai

Tokyo

Kyoto

Japan

Pacific Ocean

The Great Wall of China was built over 2,000 years ago to keep out enemies. It winds 2,414 km across the hills of northern China.

Rice is grown in paddy fields. These are fields that are flooded by the rains or by rivers.

The South Korean flag

Taipei

Taiwan

Hong Kong

The North Korean flag

Bears and a few giant pandas live in the southwest of China.

A sixth of the world's population lives in China.

River Amur

ing

| 3500 | 4000 | 4500 | 5000 | 5500 | 6000 | KM |

Australia and New Zealand

Australia is the smallest continent in the world. It lies in the southern Pacific Ocean, on the opposite side of the world from Europe. New Zealand is 1,500 km southeast of Australia. Most of Australia is flat and dry. New Zealand is more hilly and green.

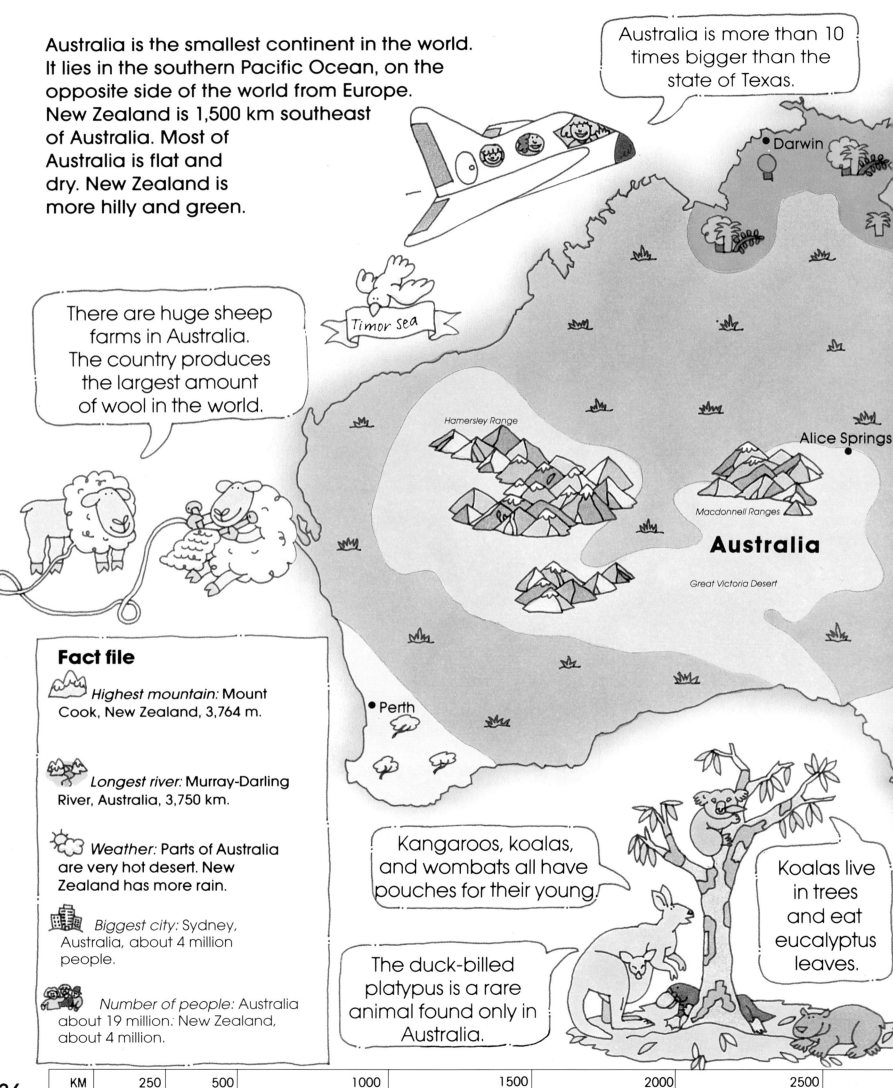

Australia is more than 10 times bigger than the state of Texas.

There are huge sheep farms in Australia. The country produces the largest amount of wool in the world.

Timor Sea

Darwin

Hamersley Range

Alice Springs

Macdonnell Ranges

Australia

Great Victoria Desert

Perth

Fact file

Highest mountain: Mount Cook, New Zealand, 3,764 m.

Longest river: Murray-Darling River, Australia, 3,750 km.

Weather: Parts of Australia are very hot desert. New Zealand has more rain.

Biggest city: Sydney, Australia, about 4 million people.

Number of people: Australia about 19 million; New Zealand, about 4 million.

Kangaroos, koalas, and wombats all have pouches for their young.

Koalas live in trees and eat eucalyptus leaves.

The duck-billed platypus is a rare animal found only in Australia.

KM	250	500	1000	1500	2000	2500

The Great Barrier Reef is the biggest coral reef in the world.

Many interesting plants and fish live on and around coral reefs.

Surfing is a popular sport in Australia.

The Aborigines were the first people to settle in Australia. They used to hunt and fight with boomerangs.

N
W E
S

Cairns

The Great Barrier Reef

Great Dividing Range

River Darling

River Murray

Adelaide

Brisbane

Sydney

Canberra

Melbourne

Tasman Sea

Hobart

Tasmania

The Australian flag

New Zealand

New Zealand has two islands called North Island and South Island.

NORTH ISLAND

Auckland

The kiwi is one of the national emblems of New Zealand. It cannot fly.

Wellington

Christchurch

The New Zealand flag

SOUTH ISLAND

	3500		4000	KM

KM	250	500	1000	KM

The Arctic

The Arctic is the area around the North Pole. It is frozen ocean surrounded by land. The ocean is covered with ice that slowly drifts from place to place.

The Icelandic flag

Polar bears live on the frozen sea. They catch seals to eat.

Alaska

Arctic Ocean

North Pole

Arctic Ocean

Russia

Canada

Greenland

Iceland

Arctic Circle

Sweden

Finland

Norway

The Inuit live in the Arctic parts of Canada, Alaska, and Greenland.

In summer, most of the Arctic land is covered with plants. Grass and mosses grow there and many flowers bloom.

KM	250	500	1000	1500	2000	2500	3000	3500	4000	4500	KM

The Antarctic

The Antarctic is ice-covered land around the South Pole. The ice is 4,500 meters thick in some places. There are many high mountains and some volcanoes.

At the North and South Poles, winter and summer last six months each. Winter is dark all day and night. In summer it is light all the time.

The Arctic

The Antarctic

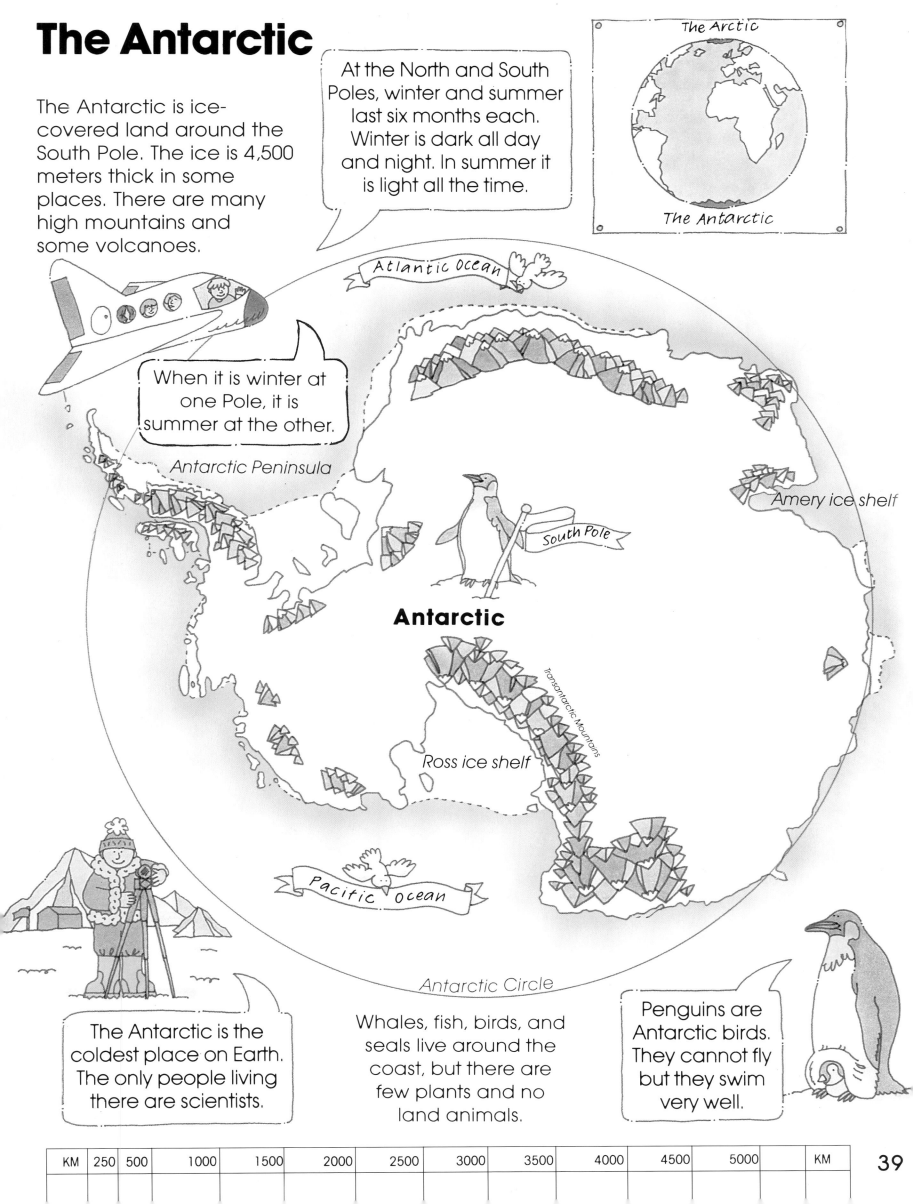

Atlantic Ocean

When it is winter at one Pole, it is summer at the other.

Antarctic Peninsula

Amery ice shelf

South Pole

Antarctic

Transantarctic Mountains

Ross ice shelf

Pacific Ocean

Antarctic Circle

The Antarctic is the coldest place on Earth. The only people living there are scientists.

Whales, fish, birds, and seals live around the coast, but there are few plants and no land animals.

Penguins are Antarctic birds. They cannot fly but they swim very well.

KM	250	500	1000	1500	2000	2500	3000	3500	4000	4500	5000	KM

Index

This book was created and produced by Zigzag, an imprint of Chrysalis Books Limited, 8, Blenheim Court, Brewery Road, London N7 2NT, UK A member of the Chrysalis Group plc.

Map consultants: Sussex University Map Library
Geography consultant: Diane Snowden

Colour separations by RCS Graphics Ltd, Leeds.
Printed and bound in Hong Kong

© 1994 Zigzag Publishing Ltd.
Revised edition © 2000 Chrysalis Books Ltd.
This edition published by Whitecap Books Ltd.,
351 Lynn Avenue, North Vancouver,
British Columbia V7J 2C4

Canadian Cataloguing in Publication Data

Wright, Nicola
Kids' Canadian Atlas

Previous ed. has title: My first Canadian Atlas
Includes Index.
ISBN 1-55285-149-4

1. Children's atlases. 2. Atlases, Canadian. I. Title. II. Title: My frist Canadian atlas.
G1021.W75 2000   j912   C00-910580-8